THE AUTHORITY GUIDE TO
FINANCIAL
FORECASTING FOR SMEs

Pain-free financials
for finance and planning

SIMON THOMPSON

The Authority Guide to Financial Forecasting for SMEs
Pain-free financials for finance and planning
© Simon Thompson

ISBN 978-1-909116-63-4
eISBN 978-1-909116-64-1

Published in 2016 by Authority Guides
authorityguides.co.uk

Printed in the UK by TJ International, Padstow.

Contents

Contents

Part 1

Welcome to my world

"

We forecast our businesses for two reasons only: to understand our numbers and to communicate them to others. How well a forecast helps with these is the only measure of how good it is.

"

Introduction

Since first devoting myself to a fairly unusual speciality in providing tailored forecasts for small and medium businesses back in 2011, I've built hundreds of them. But I've also reviewed and worked with even more that I *didn't* build myself, and it's those forecasts that have prompted me to write this book.

To cut a long story short, I've seen a huge range in the quality and effectiveness of these financials and, in addition, evidence of a lot of wasted time and effort spent doing it quite badly (and often worse!).

The simple fact is that although financial forecasting is an almost universal requirement for any small business at some point in its life, there seems to be a lack of clear, simple guidance on what's required, how it works and how to go about it. As a result, far too many businesses routinely get it wrong.

I want to help you to avoid those pitfalls, so I'll distil what I've learnt over many years of building financial projections and share the essence of the rules, benchmarks and best practice I've established to create more effective forecasts in less time and with less pain.

> A forecast is a picture of a financial journey, and you can't make sense of a journey unless you know where you're starting from. Clear, recent, and materially correct opening balances are a must.

Is this book for you?

This book is for just about anyone in a small or medium business who needs to 'do some numbers'.

It shares underlying principles and golden rules which I have found apply to virtually all businesses regardless of size or aims. From a tiny start-up to a £5–10 million owner-managed business; from a simple cash flow projection for a £1,000 start-up loan to a full financial model for a big crowdfunding pitch; or just to run the numbers on your business plan, whether you're a sole trader or a limited company, this book is for you.

You'll find the advice it gives is equally valid whether you're building your own forecast model from scratch or using off-the-shelf spreadsheet templates or software. Even if you're outsourcing the whole job to an accountant or consultant (like me!), you'll be better equipped to procure the work and make sure you get value for money and the result you need.

"

If you're in business for the long haul, sooner or later you're going to have to get your head around the meaning of profit & loss, cash flow *and* balance sheet...

"

How will this book help?

This book will:

- teach you the underlying principles of good 'small business' forecasting
- help you to make better decisions about how you go about this task
- save you time (and money) in executing it
- make sure you produce a more useful, professional result to give you a better chance of getting your finance.

It will shine a light on:

- why you forecast and what you need to achieve
- the essential benchmarks of all good forecasts
- a foolproof ten-step process that you can apply to nail your numbers in the shortest time.

The overall aim of this book is simple: to help you achieve the most effective financial forecast in the minimum time. And let's be clear: 'effective' means a forecast that will help you get your money!

This book isn't a 'manual'. It doesn't prescribe a specific tool for the job (although I recommend mine!) and it doesn't deal with the background spreadsheet skills and accountancy knowledge you'll need if you build your own model. (I assume that if you're going down that road you've already got those core skills.)

What it does provide is essential knowledge, tips and insights into the forecasting process that you can apply, however you go about it.

Doing it properly: profit and loss, cash flow *and* balance sheet

Whatever you're trying to do, you can always find a shortcut. Sometimes you get away with it; sometimes you don't.

This book isn't about shortcuts. Certainly it is about completing this task in the least possible time with the least possible pain, but its main concern is producing a forecast that is *complete* and *professional* and works in any circumstance; a forecast that you can have absolute confidence in, will never need to apologise for and that will always meet the needs of *any* bank or investor.

Achieving this standard in financial forecasting relies in particular on recognising the importance of the three fundamental elements of business accounting: profit and loss, cash flow and balance sheet, and that you cannot avoid the fact that each depends on the others and can't be separated. As we shall see, a cash flow that does not depend on a profit and loss, or a forecast which doesn't have a balance sheet, simply lacks integrity. You may get away with it, but that's another matter.

It is beyond the scope of this book to explain or justify this approach but it is the premise on which it's based. You may well encounter apparently simpler styles of forecast which omit one or more of these elements, and they may well be compliant in specific circumstances. But I can tell you with absolute confidence that they *will* have limitations and the potential to let you down in any number of ways.

Einstein said something along the lines of: 'keep it as simple as possible, and no simpler', and that's the case here. However simple your finances may be, your forecast needs to include all three standard accounting elements to do its job properly.

This book will show you how and why and I promise that in the long run you'll find it more logical, easier to understand and it will certainly equip you with a more professional stance to take forward in your business career.

.

Part II

Before you start

Getting to a final, finished version of your forecast can be like getting kittens in a box. You're bound to cycle through it many times and a clear, comprehensive process is key. (At least start by knowing how many kittens you've got...)

Why do we forecast?

Start with the end in mind...

It has to be said that if you're concerned with working out the best way to do something, it helps to be clear about why you're doing it in the first place; to understand what your objectives are.

We forecast in business for a mix of two reasons.

1 To *understand*. It's from a desire to understand the potential financial outcome of our business, based on the various different assumptions we may make. In essence to run the numbers; to see if the plan 'stacks'; to quantify our goals. We do it for *us*.

2 To *communicate*. We do it to communicate our financials to someone else – usually a lender or investor because we want some money from them. We do it for *them*.

In an ideal world the first precedes the second. We would always want to understand our own numbers; to know that they stack, even if we weren't after money. But in fact it's often the other way round. What causes a forecast to be built is usually an impending finance application: most often we build a forecast because we have to.

All the advice in this book is focused on these two objectives: what factors contribute to our *understanding* or our ability to *communicate* what the recipient wants to know? How well it does these two things is the only measure of a good forecasting process.

The eight essential benchmarks of all good forecasts

Financial forecasts come in all shapes and sizes. Like most jobs, all are achieved through a combination of knowledge, skills and experience, and some kind of a tool for the job.

I can tell you from experience that good forecasts will tend to share a clear set of common qualities and benchmarks. However you finally go about this task, the more of these you can achieve, the easier your life is going to be, the better the result and the more likely you are to meet your real objectives.

What's more, the odd thing about these benchmarks is that they are barely more expensive to include than to omit, and the ones that take a little more time in the short run will generally save time in the long run. They are mostly the application of common sense, and the trick is *be aware* of them. Tools and techniques to achieve them are readily available if you know what you're looking for.

Keep these benchmarks in mind when you go about your forecast!

The conventional accounting structure: profit and loss, cash flow *and* balance sheet

We've already covered this, but it bears repeating. Double-entry bookkeeping, on which these concepts are based, has been around since the 15th century. We still use it for a simple reason: it works! It is the foundation of professional business finance and it's no different because your business is small or a start-up. You need to understand it, not reinvent or ignore it.

Try not to see it as a burden. The structure of profit and loss, cash flow and balance sheet is a clever, elegant and productive way of dealing with business numbers. It's your friend, not your enemy. Make sure your forecast structure adopts it and take the time to understand how it works. It is valuable – some would say *indispensable* – business knowledge.

A good forecast always comprises profit and loss, cash flow and balance sheet.

Self-editable (*own* your numbers!)

We've all seen *Dragon's Den*. We know what happens when people don't understand their own numbers. It's never pretty! You need to be fully in control of the numbers in your forecast. (If only because they're usually subject to a surprising amount of revision before they're published. Sometimes it's like getting kittens in a box!) The only way to properly own them is to input and edit them *yourself*.

If you're outsourcing your forecast to an accountant you need to make sure that you get a model that *you* can understand and edit. Avoid the temptation to let an advisor enter numbers and just give you the finished result. Make sure you're part of that input process.

A good forecast is easy to own and edit.

Flexible

Things change in business. You think you know how it all works and then something unexpected happens, or you simply change your mind. Your forecast has to be adaptable: flexible enough to respond to changes in circumstances or expectations. This is a functional, practical consideration. Can you easily add records to your forecast? Can you edit the way you calculate certain numbers? Can you easily change the start date when time has slipped?

When either outsourcing the forecast or buying software to do it, make sure it offers this flexibility. Off-the-shelf solutions can be surprisingly restrictive about what they'll easily let you do.

A good forecast is flexible and can easily respond to changing circumstances.

Properly 'tailored'

Your forecast tells the financial side of the story you set out in your business plan. Within a conventional accounting structure it should be set up to specifically reflect your business. When you look at your forecast do you recognise the business which you are trying to manage and discuss? Or have you shoehorned it into some vague and generic business model?

A good forecast sets out a specific, recognisable business. (Yours!)

The right level of detail

There is no hard and fast rule about the level of detail required in any forecast. It depends on what you're trying to understand and what you're trying to communicate. Too much and too little detail are the twin enemies of understanding and communication. If it helps, put it in; if it doesn't contribute to either, leave it out.

A good forecast has the right level of detail. (Not too much; not too little!)

Clear, recent opening balances

Your forecast is a picture of a financial journey, and you can't describe a journey unless you know where you're starting from.

Your current financial position (and to a lesser extent at least a summary of *how* you got there) is fundamental to the integrity of your forecast. Anyone interested in your forecast, especially someone who is considering lending or investing money, is bound to ask, 'Where are you now?'

This information should be up to date, and materially correct – not months old because you haven't done your books for ages, or incorrect or incomplete because you haven't done them properly!

A good forecast shows clear, recent and materially correct opening balances.

Modelled revenue and direct costs, with clear assumptions

Sales revenue is *always* the product of activity: it doesn't come from nowhere. It is always the result of 'so many people doing so many things at an average price of…' or some variation on that theme.

A forecast which projects revenue in purely monetary terms, without addressing the extent or plausibility of this activity (How many new customers? How much will they spend?…) is rarely adequate, in terms of either your own understanding or what you need to communicate. There are some circumstances in which you can get away with it, but in general you need to understand and model what *drives* your revenue, and state your assumptions clearly.

The same is true of the financial relationships which drive your direct costs or 'cost of sales'. These are inevitably defined by their relationship to sales according to some assumption, and this needs to be modelled.

A good forecast models revenue and direct costs and shows assumptions clearly.

Clear, transparent, user-friendly reports

We've already said, numerous times, that one of the main reasons you are likely to be building a forecast is to communicate your numbers to someone else, so obviously producing reports is an important issue.

There are two sides to this. One is the amount of grief this gives you at a practical level. (Creating coherent, legible documents from extensive spreadsheets can be unbelievably time-consuming!) The other is the quality and effectiveness of what you produce – from the *reader's* perspective.

You need to be able to produce reports which are both readable and legible. By readable I mean well laid out, logically paginated and clearly labelled, and by legible I mean the right amount of information on a single page at a font size that can be read easily both on screen and when printed. And they need to be in an appropriate format (almost always a PDF file and not a raw spreadsheet file), so that they can be electronically published and distributed. They need to look professional and make a strong impression that reflects well on you and your business.

A good forecast produces user-friendly reports that are clear, elegant and professional, and makes life easy for everyone.

Conclusion

When you think about your core objectives in forecasting – to *understand* and to *communicate*, these benchmarks are just common sense. They are obviously things which make a positive contribution to these objectives. It is equally obvious that if you compromise them, you will compromise your objectives.

They are not rules. Instead, think of them as setting the bar. Use them as tests for any process or tool you may be considering or already using. You may not always achieve all of them, but the closer you get, the better your result will be.

Understanding profit and loss, cash flow and balance sheet

The terms profit and loss, cash flow and balance sheet are bandied about freely in the business world, but it is surprising how many entrepreneurs aren't really clear on exactly what these things are, how they differ and how they relate to one another. Since they are the foundation of all business finance it is essential to have at least a basic understanding of them. If you're in any doubt, here's my perspective on them, in the context of producing a good forecast.

Profit and loss

Sometimes known as the 'profit and loss account', most often referred to just as the 'P&L', and occasionally as the 'income statement' (American), the P&L measures how you do (your profitability) over a length of time. It could be any period but most commonly will refer to a month, a series of months or a single year.

The projected P&L is the basic foundation of your forecast. It is the projection of your trading activities. As we will see, your cash flow projection depends overwhelmingly on it and can't logically be calculated without an awareness of it.

In general a P&L should observe a conventional structure as follows:

	Revenue
less	Direct costs (or cost of sales)
equals	Gross profit
less	Overheads (or 'fixed costs' or 'operating expenses')
equals	Earnings before interest, tax, depreciation and amortisation (EBITDA)
less	Interest and depreciation
equals	Net profit/(loss)

Any professional P&L will more or less follow this structure, but be aware that some terms can be quite loosely interpreted.

In summary, the P&L shows you how well you did. It provides a proper accounting view of your income and expenditure in a period, regardless of when you pay or get paid for things. In respect of your forecast it represents the largest part of what you will input and its values will have a major impact on the resulting calculations for cash flow and balance sheet.

You can see an example 12 monthly P&L in the demonstration forecast report downloadable from www.edgeforecast.co.uk/demo

Cash flow

For any month your cash flow projection will take an opening cash balance, add to it all receipts, deduct all payments and calculate a closing balance. It will then carry this balance forward to the next month and start again. What it shows is the running balance of available cash through the life of the business.

Projecting your overall cash flow relies on two things. The first is the input of specific ad hoc transactions: for example, the receipt of a bank loan or investment funds, which are usually individual, direct inputs – you type a single number into a single cell or box. This is quite straightforward to deal with.

The second is by definition a *calculation* based on a variety of other things. When projecting sales cash flow, for example, you need to know the projection for invoiced sales in a period, the assumption about how long you may wait for payment, whether or not it will include value-added tax (VAT) and possibly a consideration of what you are owed by customers at the start of the process. And that calculation in itself will impact the calculation for the VAT payment or receipt some months down the line. All this can vary greatly in complexity depending on specifics, so you must be aware of how complex or simple your circumstances are.

Assuming your chosen method is capable of allowing you to input the major ad hoc payments and receipts, and also models your trading cash flow adequately, you need to make sure it is *comprehensive*. You must cover a finite list of receipt and payment types, *although some may not apply in your individual circumstances*.

Receipt types are likely to include:

- Equity investment, or, if a sole trader, owner contributions (or 'capital introduced').
- Directors' loans.
- Other loans (shareholder loans, inter-company and other ad hoc loans).
- Bank loans and other institutional finance, or grants.
- Sales receipts from 'opening' debtors (or 'receivables').

- Sales receipts from projected sales.
- VAT refunds.
- Research and development (R&D) tax credits.

Payment types are likely to include:

- Payments to opening creditors (or 'payables').
- Payments for projected direct costs and overheads.
- Capital expenditure.
- Net wages payments (after deductions).
- Statutory payments to Her Majesty's Revenue and Customs (HMRC) (VAT, Pay As You Earn (PAYE), corporation tax).
- Loan repayments.
- Dividends (or, if a sole trader, 'drawings').

In summary, the cash flow sets out to project the movements of cash in and out of the business, and the running balance, with a view to establishing that the business has enough cash at any point to carry out what it's projecting to do. By definition it should be largely a calculation based on other inputs, and not an input in itself.

You can see an example 12 monthly cash flow in the demon-stration forecast report downloadable from www.edgeforecast. co.uk/demo

Balance sheet

Whether historic or projected, the primary purpose of a balance sheet is to present the overall financial position of a business at *a single point in time*. This is what distinguishes it from the P&L, which describes *how you performed over a period* (whether it's a month, a year or any other length of time). It shows *where you are*. It will inevitably accompany a P&L to show the position you have reached at the end of that period of trading.

A balance sheet first of all sets out a list of your assets and liabilities: the net total of everything you have (or are owed) and everything you owe. This is one way of summarising your overall financial position and is known as your 'net assets and liabilities'.

One way or another your balance sheet should adopt more or less the following structure and contain the items listed below.

Assets

- Fixed assets (the 'written-down' value of assets, after depreciation to date)
- Current assets, including:
  - Cash and bank balances
  - Trade debtors (or receivables, i.e. customers who owe you money)
  - Other debtors (including overdrawn directors' loan accounts)
  - Current stocks
  - Prepayments and work in progress

Added together these are your 'total assets'.

Liabilities

- Current liabilities:
  - Overdrawn bank accounts
  - Trade creditors (or payables, i.e. suppliers who you owe money to)
  - Statutory liabilities (VAT, PAYE, corporation tax)
  - Bank loans

- o Directors', shareholder and other loans
- Long-term liabilities:
  - o Loans and so on due after 12 months

Added together these are your 'total liabilities'.

Total assets less your total liabilities equals your 'net assets/(liabilities)'.

Shareholders' funds (the balancing bit…)

The second part of a balance sheet adds together two elements:

- The total *equity* in the business – the amount that has been invested in it via shares (which could be as little as that £1 share you issued yourself when you incorporated your business, or could include any other shares you have sold).
- The *profit and loss reserves* – the total cumulative amount of profit (or loss), after tax, which is retained in the business, that is, has not been lost to taxation or distributed via dividend to shareholders.

Added together, these are normally referred to as 'shareholders' funds', 'shareholders' equity' or sometimes 'net worth'. This shows the total financial value of the business at this point.

The magic bit is that if your bookkeeping (or your projection model) has been done properly your net assets and liabilities and your shareholders' funds will always balance. It does this by relying on the principle of double-entry bookkeeping, which I'm not going to try to explain here, but trust me works!

Crucially, in respect of a forecast it is important to recognise that there is nothing for you to *input* into a balance sheet: it can only be *calculated* on the basis of what happens in the P&L and cash flow.

Making a balance sheet work is often a major chore for people building their own models but in purpose-built software you can more or less rely on a balance sheet adding up properly. (If it doesn't you really have bought a dud!) What you won't be able to control is the level of transparency and elegance with which it presents information, and this can be quite variable.

You can see an example 12 monthly balance sheet in the demonstration forecast report downloadable from www.edgeforecast.co.uk/demo

Time to get on with it...

In this part of the book I have tried to give you an understanding of what underpins the whole thing – to remind you why you're doing it, what you need to achieve and to signpost ways of doing it well.

In the next part we will look at how to break the process down into ten logical, manageable chunks. You can apply this process however you choose to build your forecast, and we'll look at the most common practical issues you will face in each of them.

Before you start I recommend you download the demonstration forecast report from www.edgeforecast.co.uk/demo This report will illustrate the majority of the principles I promote in this book and will show you what the final output may look like if they have been applied.

OK, enough musing and philosophising. It's time to get on with the job in hand!

There are no bad answers, just different answers. They apply to every business large or small, and once you know them you need to think about how it applies to your business and whether you need to act on it. You should carry out a financial review of your business.

Part III

Ten logical, comprehensive steps to a great forecast

"

Whatever you're trying to do, you can always find a shortcut. Sometimes you get away with it; sometimes you don't.

"

An introduction to the ten steps

When I began to specialise in financial forecasting (I used to be a general bookkeeper and management accountant in between bouts of entrepreneurship), I adopted a fairly instinctive approach to it, based on experience, which seemed to get the job done. At the same time I built the first version of the spreadsheet software that allowed me to do this and provide my clients with an editable, tailored forecast.

In the following years I became increasingly analytical about the process – mostly because I needed to become more efficient at it. What I came to realise was that I inevitably went through the same steps, in more or less the same order, and that the more I kept to this orderly path, the more efficient it became. And most importantly: it *always* worked; everything got covered.

I have now refined this process into ten clear, separate steps that I use every time I build a forecast, and I can promise the task is hugely more manageable once broken down like this. In fact, it never fails. But before we explore the steps so you can apply them yourself there's a few things you need to know about them.

They are universal...

These steps apply to *every* forecast, regardless of the size, complexity or aims of a business. What differs from business to business is simply the scale, significance or complexity of each step. This is true for every step.

They are comprehensive...

They will cover *everything* you need to address, although some may be insignificant or not applicable in your particular case. They are a reliable checklist, and together they effectively constitute a complete financial review of your business.

The order you do them in isn't crucial...

Although they appear in a logical order, and indeed they're best gone through in this order at least once, the nature of forecasting as a task is that you tend to cycle through these things, going over bits and revising and refining them.

They won't always look exactly like this in purpose-built spreadsheets or software... (except mine!)

Not everyone sees life the way I do. Some may organise this process differently, or use different terms. What I *can* tell you is that each of these steps is a necessary part of the process and must be present *somewhere* in every tool or method or you risk missing something.

Step 1: The global considerations

At the start of any process like this are the global considerations that define the overall scope of what you're doing. Running through them and understanding them should always be the first step in any forecast, whether you are trying to choose a piece of software or attempting to build one yourself. Ask: how well will your proposed solution deal with these global issues?

In purpose-built software and spreadsheets you will have very little discretion in how these things are handled. In theory you can painstakingly evaluate these potential solutions before you proceed but this is not very realistic. In practice the best you can hope for is a sense that it is likely to meet your needs, but you may later experience a degree of frustration when it comes to what it will and won't let you do and how it handles things. Welcome to the real world of forecasting software!

The issues to consider appear below.

Allowing for inflation or forecasting at 'current values'

It is generally accepted in forecasting at this level that you do so at 'current values'. This means that you take no account of inflation. You avoid bothering *at all* with something that is in any case difficult to predict, but the principal advantage is that it aids comparison – you are comparing year to year on equal terms.

Otherwise you need to factor in a consistent and plausible inflation policy throughout the forecast. (Best avoided!)

Forecast start date

In answer to the question, 'When should my forecast start?' the short answer is 'this month'. But life isn't always so simple.

If you have absolutely no financial history before the start of your forecast, then the start should be either this month or at whatever point in the future you expect your financial activity to start.

If you have *any* relevant financial history – however small, and even if you are still 'pre-revenue' – your forecast should start with a clear view of your current financial position. Your forecast should therefore start immediately after the most recent point at which you can provide this information (usually referred to as your 'opening balance sheet' or 'opening balances'). Clearly to be useful this should be as recent as possible – in practice ideally the end of last month – but this may be affected by the availability of up-to-date accounting information.

Be aware also that between embarking on the forecasting process and actually publishing reports for some purpose, some months may have passed and later you may need to adjust the start date of your forecast to reflect this. Forecasts with a start date that is obviously some way in the past do not make the best impression, and they invite the question: 'do the figures for months already passed reflect what actually happened?'

Avoid using the headers 'month 1, month 2' and so on, except where you have no opening balances and are unsure when financial activity will start. Otherwise all this achieves is a lack of clarity around the timing of your projections.

The length and time frame of the forecast

Don't make a forecast any longer than is truly useful. Projections, as we all know, become quite dubious pretty quickly and even years two and three are rarely more than a guess in a party dress. Extending to four and five years is of dubious benefit and is certainly only useful at a very summary level, and not in any detail that it may purport to show. Some lenders and investors insist on it of course, so you may have no choice.

Your forecast should almost always be arranged in consistent 12 month periods to aid comparison (most purpose-built software will dictate this) and aligning your forecast with your formal accounting period or calendar years is usually of little significance.

Modelling cash flow

The ability of your forecast to model your cash flow characteristics adequately is crucial to its effectiveness. In particular, one of the key things that affects your cash flow is the assumption made about the delay in payment for individual lines of revenue and expense. You therefore need to consider whether your chosen solution allows you to reflect the nature of the payment terms you are likely to be faced with, especially if you are likely to need to explore the cash flow outcome of applying different payment terms to different things.

In many cases a simple relationship in respect of, say, a one month delay for payment is quite easy to model and available in most software solutions. However, if you have more complex arrangements you are almost bound to need to build your own forecast spreadsheet. For example, an importer of goods from the Far East may need to model the payment of a deposit several months in advance of shipping, payment of the duty and VAT in the month when the goods are received and the balance of the invoice then or later. Few forecast software solutions I've ever seen would allow you to do this.

Make sure your forecast's functionality for modelling cash flow is adequate for your reality.

VAT

Remember that core business financials (P&L and balance sheet) are always expressed *exclusive* of VAT. The primary significance of VAT for a forecast is how it impacts cash flow. Payments and receipts (for a VAT-registered business) will include VAT, and therefore many cash flow values will differ from the P&L values to which they relate by 20 per cent, and the cash impact on the resulting periodic VAT return can be substantial. Thus while VAT has no bearing on P&L, it is usually considered to have a material impact on cash flow and therefore needs to be a fundamental part of your forecast.

Apart from its effect on cash flow, being VAT registered also gives rise to an inevitable liability (or sometimes a debtor balance) which needs to be recognised on your balance sheet.

Having said all that however, the operation of VAT is very complex in the real world and it rarely benefits us to attempt to mirror this complexity in a forecast model. Generally speaking most purpose-built software will treat VAT on a basic, quarterly accrual basis and this is usually adequate. (You may find some that will allow for 'cash accounting' as an alternative.) Your specific circumstances may dictate that you need to model the effect of specific VAT arrangements, but only you can say whether such things are material to your projections. If so, you need to make sure your solution can accommodate it.

Stock

If you buy in goods – either to manufacture something or simply to resell them – you will almost certainly have an issue about projecting the financial implications of stock (or 'inventory').

The significance of stock to your forecast is that in profit and loss terms the expense of these goods in any period (known as the 'cost of goods sold') is *specifically* the cost of what was *sold* in that period, *not* what was *purchased*. Cash flow, on the other hand, is entirely driven by what is *purchased* (and when it has to be paid for), and there is a further concern on the balance sheet about the value of stock at any point.

As a result therefore, your forecast solution must include a stock model which allows you to predict or enter the level and timing of your stock purchases, recognise the costs of goods sold in any period and show you the resulting figure for what is tied up in stock at any point.

Businesses vary hugely in how significant an issue stock is to their financial model and forecast software varies equally in its sophistication around handling it. You should make sure that yours does what it needs to do.

Payroll and PAYE

Most expenses in your forecast are assumed to be on an 'invoiced' basis. You project an expense in a period, make an assumption about any delay in payment and whether it has VAT on it, and your forecast will calculate the resulting cash flow and the impact on your creditors' position.

Payroll expenses behave differently and you may wish to cater for this within your forecast.

Under the rules of PAYE, payments to employees for wages or salaries are subject to the deduction of tax and National Insurance, and you will have to administer these as an employer and pay over to HMRC, normally the following month.

This gives rise not only to some specific cash flow behaviour, but also a separate 'liability' (for the deductions yet to be paid over) at any point in time which needs to be included in your balance sheet.

However, especially since the cash flow of payroll (under normal circumstances) will always 'wash out' within a month, you may feel that it is not worth reflecting this cash flow in your model. You would need to decide whether the difference in the effect on overall cash flow between paying, say, 70 per cent of your payroll bill one month and then 30 per cent to PAYE the next, compared with paying 100 per cent in the first month, was material in your case.

One thing that is worth noting in respect of payroll costs is the issue of 'Employer's National Insurance' contributions. People tend to think in terms of gross salary when projecting payroll expense, but any salary (above the National Insurance threshold) will also cost the employer a premium in terms of employer's National Insurance. For example, a typical £20,000 salary currently attracts an additional £1,662 per annum in employer's National Insurance. Be sure to bear this additional cost in mind when setting your budgets!

Other than providing for this material additional cost (which need only be an approximation), you should avoid attempting to replicate the precision of tax bands and rates in projected figures. The overall margin for error in any forecast is considerable, and the idea of trying to project this one area in so much detail is futile. If you come across someone who thinks this is worth bothering with, then you've found someone who doesn't understand what a forecast is for or what it is capable of. Please lend them this book.

Bank interest

Particularly if you are forecasting that you will be likely to have an overdraft at any point in the forecast, you will need to have a provision to calculate overdraft interest with an editable input for the interest rate.

You may feel inclined to allow for an interest rate which varies over time, perhaps to forecast for a general increasing trend, but this is probably overkill in most circumstances (except where interest is a significant expense) and it's not in accord with my general advice to forecast at current values.

You may also wish to project for interest received, perhaps with a threshold below which no interest is received.

If you are being strictly correct your P&L should be structured to show interest as a separate line below what is known as the EBITDA. Whether you adhere to this is dependent on the level of accountancy professionalism you are aiming at.

Current and long-term liabilities

In formal accounting, a distinction is usually made between 'current' and 'long-term' liabilities on a balance sheet. Current liabilities are those due or projected to be repaid within 12 months. (Long-term liabilities clearly are those due after 12 months.)

The significance of this distinction is that it affects a view of what is known as the 'liquidity' of the business, or in other words its ability to meet its short-term commitments: the greater the level of current liabilities, the greater the pressure to balance those liabilities with short-term assets (cash and debtors etc.) in order to pay them 'as and when they fall due'.

You will need to decide whether such a distinction is material in your circumstances and, if it is, to make sure that the forecast solution you choose allows for it. It is often the case that in smaller businesses the additional complexity involved in addressing it within the model (especially if you're building your own) doesn't really add much to the clarity of the overall financial information, but for some it may be significant. If in doubt, ask an accountant!

Corporation tax

Assuming you're a limited company (this section can be ignored if you're not) and you intend to present a balance sheet as part of your financials, you should probably make sure you include a provisional corporation tax liability since it potentially represents a significant item in your cash flow and a significant reduction to the overall net worth of your business at any point.

Just as with PAYE, however, there is little point in attempting a detailed corporation tax calculation. A simple provision will usually do, probably based on the basic rate of tax applied to your overall net profit, rather than attempting to predict the likely adjustments such as disallowable expenses and capital allowances.

In the relatively rare circumstances in which you are predicting a corporation tax *refund*, you may encounter difficulties as I have rarely seen purpose-built software which deals with this elegantly. Most even struggle with the concept of 'brought forward losses for corporation tax purposes' which affects the projected calculation.

Such are the complexities of corporation tax that many forecasts just choose to ignore it, and recognise that there is a liability without trying to quantify it, and there's something to be said for this approach. If you're really concerned about it, talk to an accountant.

R&D tax credits

R&D tax credits are a form of funding provided by HMRC to incentivise speculative expenditure which seeks to achieve some kind of technological advance.

If you are trading profitably (and therefore incurring tax), this is likely to give rise to a reduction in your tax bill, and therefore is simply a consideration in the arguments above about whether or not to attempt to mirror its complexities within your model, or (and it's very unlikely) whether your chosen software will handle it.

In some circumstances, however – and this often happens after an early period of incurring expense on R&D – you may be entitled to a cash refund which is a material part of your cash flow and you may want to show it. The simplest way to deal with this is to treat it as an additional revenue stream. In accounting terms this is not strictly correct – since your model will probably treat this as 'sales' revenue in your P&L statement – but in practical terms, provided you ensure it is transparent, and clearly noted somewhere, it is adequate for most purposes. It is after all, to all intents and purposes, just some additional revenue.

Summary

These 'global considerations' have a considerable, practical impact on the process of forecasting, and being aware of them is a vital first step in any forecast. Make sure you identify which ones are significant to you and what level of detail and sophistication you need to apply to them. Think them through thoroughly before you try to either source a piece of purpose-built software or build one yourself.

Step 2: The chart of accounts

The 'chart of accounts' is just a fancy name for the list of revenue and expense items you have in your business, and how they're arranged. The more elegant and logical the structure of this list, the easier it will be to work with for both the forecaster and their reader. The chart is also important because it effectively defines exactly *what* we are forecasting and – crucially – at what level of detail.

For this reason it is well worth going through this step *before* you start work, as opposed to more randomly creating the list and its structure as you go.

For our purposes we will consider the chart of accounts to comprise the following elements:

- Revenue streams
- Direct costs
- Overheads
- Asset types
- Individual loan accounts

In purpose-built software you will find varying levels of control over the chart of accounts and you may or may not be led to deal with it naturally at the beginning of the process. A lot of software seems to encourage you to create accounts *as you populate them*, which is not as efficient or reliable as concentrating on it as a single task.

The first three of these elements (revenue, direct costs and overheads) define the major part of your P&L structure. The rest of your P&L is made up of the expenses for the depreciation for each of your asset types and interest incurred (or occasionally earned) for any loans to (or from) your business.

The key qualities of an effective chart of accounts

Keep the following things in mind when creating your chart of accounts.

The right level of detail

A good chart of accounts has a level of detail which is relevant and useful to you, and to your audience. For example, only you can say whether a single line of overhead for 'premises costs' is adequate in your circumstances or whether it would be better shown as individual lines for 'rent', 'rates', 'utilities' and so on.

A logical elegant structure

Lists of any kind are easier to work with if they are logically and elegantly constructed.

It is preferable to make sure that you gather the detailed lines into groups of associated items, which helps with the sense that nothing has been forgotten (it goes without saying that your chart of accounts must be comprehensive and leave nothing important out) and also helps when it comes to subtotalling cost centres for more concise reporting.

Remember also that your chart of accounts should observe the conventional P&L structure in respect of 'revenue less direct costs equals gross profit, less overheads equals net profit'.

Clear, understandable descriptions

* Be consistent with how you describe things in written plans and discussions. Don't say 'consultancy sales' in your financials if your written plan calls it 'professional services'

* Describe the 'nature' of an account, that is, what it does. For example say 'packaging costs' rather than 'Jenkins and Co' because that's the name of the supplier you expect to use (which would mean nothing to someone who didn't know them)

* Avoid any kind of jargon or unintelligible abbreviations

* Always ask if someone who didn't know your business would automatically understand from its description what every line item related to

The significance of 'direct costs' and 'gross profit'

There is one particular issue in the arrangement of a chart of accounts which sometimes causes confusion. In broad terms, a business has two different measures of profitability. Gross profit is the profit you make from your product or service, after you deduct all the *direct* costs of doing it. Net profit is what you're left with after you've deducted all your overheads and other expenses from your gross profit.

What's important about gross profit is that it shows you the inherent profitability of whatever you do or sell. It follows that in order to have a clear measure of gross profit we need a clear definition of 'direct' costs. Unfortunately in practice this definition can be a little imprecise (to say the least), even amongst accountants, and especially amongst others who haven't paused to consider what the purpose of measuring gross profit is. You therefore need to get clear in your mind what you consider your 'direct' costs to be.

Some accountants wouldn't necessarily agree with me, but I believe that everyone is better off pursuing a straightforward definition of a direct cost which is:

A cost which is only incurred when you make a sale.

This would mean that you would include things like your cost of goods sold for something you resell, or credit card payment commission, delivery costs and sales commissions (no sale, no cost), but would exclude things like speculative marketing expenditure, or any allocation of overheads or more 'fixed' costs.

The acid test is: if you set your revenue to zero, your direct costs would be zero (no sale, no cost). Of course life is sometimes not so simple; it is up to you to define what you wish to include and you may have advisors who have specific views on the subject. In the end it's a matter of opinion, not fact, and what isn't included in direct costs goes into overheads.

One cost which doesn't always meet our neat definition, but which is often included in direct costs, is 'direct wages'. This tends to be rather more 'fixed' in its nature (which is to say that even if sales dried up you would probably still have to meet this cost at least in the short term). It usually refers to employees who are directly involved in the production or delivery of your product or service.

Chart of accounts – key points

- An elegant, logically structured chart of accounts really helps you when you work with your numbers, and is vital to help your reader make sense of them. Take the time to create it before you start putting numbers into your forecast

- Use a standard, conventional accounting structure

- Make sure you give every account a clear, transparent and self-explanatory name

- A clear understanding of what to include in your direct costs is vital to establishing a clear sense of gross profitability

"

Sales revenue doesn't appear out of nowhere. It's always the result of some kind of activity. (So many people buying so many things etc.) Sorry, but you can't just stick a number in.

"

Step 3: Opening balances

Why are they important?

A forecast shows a financial journey over time, and you can't describe a journey unless you know where you're starting from. If you think about it (and it's amazing how many people don't!), the first thing any reader of your forecast ought to want to know is 'What is the current financial position?' This means that a clear understanding of it is a must.

How accurate and detailed do they need to be?

If you are a pure start-up – that is, you have *no* meaningful financial history at all – then you can relax for now and go make a cup of tea. Your opening balances are clearly zero. That makes them simple and easy. But for anyone else this requirement brings sharply into focus the thorny issue of your bookkeeping.

Keeping up-to-date, reliable accounts is often neither a priority nor a strength for a small business. If you're an exception to this, well done, and I'm not here to lecture anyone on the need to bother with this tedious stuff, simply to point out that, unfortunately, it's a prerequisite for the job in hand.

For quite recent periods you will inevitably be producing what are known as 'management accounts'. Whether or not this information is generated internally by your own bookkeeping processes or on your behalf by an accountant or bookkeeper, you need to decide how detailed and accurate it needs to be. This will vary according to your circumstances, but the question you need to ask is: 'Do these figures represent a clear, complete and materially correct view of my current financial position?' or maybe 'If I were considering providing loan or investment funds to this company would this information tell me what I wanted to know as a starting point?'

Where will your opening balance information come from?

Strictly speaking 'opening balances' refers to the 'opening balance sheet' – your list of assets and liabilities, balanced with your 'equity and reserves'. This is what represents your financial 'position', and technically it is all that a forecast needs as a valid starting point. However, the term is routinely used to also include a historic P&L, which simply shows your recent performance (usually for the period since your last published accounts, or your start-up, whichever is the more recent) and which is effectively for information and won't impact your forecast in any way.

By definition, you will provide this information in only one of two ways. If you use an 'accounts package' (e.g. Sage, Xero, QuickBooks, etc.), you are working with a tool that will potentially provide you with the figures you need, since it will be a 'double-entry' system and will deliver both a historic P&L and a related balance sheet. But *only* (and I stress the *only*) if your bookkeeping is up to date and incorporates any number of accounting adjustments which might have been necessary to complete the figures (such as 'wages journals', depreciation journals', 'interest accruals', etc.).

The data itself is likely to come in the form of a standard accounting report that is known as a 'trial balance': a list of figures for every account within the chart of accounts, at a specific point in time (i.e. the day before your forecast starts). If you are turning to a bookkeeper or accountant for this information ask them for a 'trial balance'.

Alternatively, if your bookkeeping is kept on spreadsheets it is what we would call 'single entry', that is, it's effectively just lists of figures (income and expenses, etc.) and almost certainly does not produce a balance sheet, so you will need to create one. Just remember that the balance sheet and the P&L relate directly to one another, and they have to 'balance', which can be the tricky bit when working from a single-entry system.

For an example of a good balance sheet structure put into practice you can download a demonstration forecast report from www.edgeforecast.co.uk/demo

Opening balances – key points

- Recognise that if you have any financial history in your business prior to your forecast start date, you need to establish your opening financial position, however simple or complex this might be. This is known as your 'opening balance sheet'

- This rarely needs to be an 'audited' position, correct to the penny. You simply need to provide information which is 'materially correct'. What constitutes 'materially correct' is a matter for your own judgement and conscience

- If your books are kept in an accounting package (Sage, Xero, QuickBooks, etc.) and the data is up to date and complete this data can be exported as a 'trial balance' report

- Your opening balance sheet should be expressed in a conventional format, and if you just have spreadsheet records expect it to be more complex to establish these figures. Remember that a balance sheet includes elements which have to 'balance' with the P&L history to date

- You may wish (or be expected) to include some historic P&L information, to show how your trading performance brought you to this point

Step 4: Capital expenditure

Capital expenditure relates to the purchase of 'assets' in your business. Assets are those things you need to equip yourself with in order to carry out your business. Assets can be classed as 'tangible', like a vehicle or a computer or property, or 'intangible', like goodwill or designs, copyrights, patents or software systems. (Think of intangible assets as things that you can't physically touch.)

The purchase of assets is distinct from other general expenses – such as your telephone bill or accountancy costs which, once incurred, are of no remaining value to you. (Such expenses appear in your P&L and are said to be 'written off'.)

It is not crucial that you consider 'capex' before you start to forecast the rest of your activities, but since you have to do it at some point you may as well ask: *'Before* I go about my business from here, is there anything I need to buy to equip myself to do it?' In practice of course, you may well revise your capital expenditure budgets later in the light of what other aspects of your forecast tell you, and indeed you may just choose to defer this whole step until later, but an early consideration of it is no bad thing.

Whenever you choose to do it, it is helpful to have a basic understanding of what defines it and what the accounting issues are, especially if you are building your own model. Like all aspects of business finances, capital expenditure is in theory subject to many accounting rules and 'standards', the fine detail of which need not really concern you at this level.

The basic issues that may affect you in the context of a small business forecast are below.

Understanding whether something is a 'capital' item

Usually the idea of an 'asset' is straightforward. Most often they are physical 'things': a desk, a computer, a car or a building, for example. It is obvious that if you spend £1,000 on a computer, you have £1,000 less in the bank, but you have an item worth £1,000. Your overall financial position is unchanged. Clearly, a computer that you own is an asset.

However, it is a fairly common error for small businesses to include 'office equipment' and other assets in the P&L. Consider that if you include the cost of this computer in your overheads, your books would show a net profit or loss *worsened* to the tune of £1,000, and your books would not recognise that in fact you own an asset worth £1,000, neither of which would be correct.

It is also important to understand that if you rent or lease something usually classed as an asset this does not represent capital expenditure, since in no sense do you own anything of any value. The regular rental payments are an overhead expense. One obvious example is the contract hiring of vehicles, but the option can apply to all sorts of equipment, and even computer software. In addition, the cost of *repairing* equipment or property (or indeed maintaining software) is an overhead, not a capital expense.

If you feel you need a more detailed analysis of what constitutes a capital expense you should ask an accountant about your specific circumstances, but the following lists show the most common things which are likely to be considered to represent capital expenditure.

Tangible items can include:

- Computers and other electronic equipment
- Office fittings and furniture
- Buildings and land
- Property improvements (as opposed to maintenance)
- Plant and equipment
- Vehicles

Intangible items can include:

- Goodwill
- Leasehold premiums (as distinct from regular rent)
- Intellectual property such as:
  - Websites and software systems (usually defined as revenue generating in the long term)
  - Designs, patents, copyrights and so on

Generally you will divide your capital expenditure into 'classes' of assets, distinguishing between, for example, plant and machinery, office equipment and motor vehicles. This is partly to make the nature of your capital expenditure more transparent for both you and your reader, but also because different classes of asset are likely to be subject to different rates of 'depreciation', which we will discuss next.

Depreciation and amortisation

How depreciation works

There is of course a genuine expense to the business in respect of most assets and that is the rate at which they wear out or lose their value. We call this expense 'depreciation' (or 'amortisation' in the case of intangible assets, although the two terms are often mixed up) and, especially if you are building your own forecast model, you need to understand how it is established.

Consider our £1,000 computer. We think it may have a useful life of three years at the most, by when it will be virtually worthless. We therefore decide it is appropriate to 'depreciate' it at a rate of 33.3 per cent per year. For three years, therefore, our forecast model would make a provision for an expense to the business (called 'office equipment depreciation') of £333 in the P&L, and record an equivalent entry to reduce the value of the asset by the same sum. (Welcome to the world of double-entry bookkeeping!)

The rate and basis of depreciation

It is rarely possible to predict precisely the rate at which something loses its value, and it rarely does so in an orderly fashion. Thus calculating depreciation (whether in projections or actual bookkeeping) is a matter of making a *provision*. Accounting standards dictate that we do this on the basis of a reasonable assessment of the 'useful life' of the asset and there are two methods for the calculation. The first is 'straight line', where the asset is 'written down' in equal steps until it is deemed to be worthless (on the books). The second is 'reducing balance', where a percentage provision is successively applied to the gradually reducing balance.

Because depreciation is just a provision it is rarely considered a material figure in accounts, and indeed interested parties will often virtually ignore depreciation in a P&L, and expect to see a figure expressed for the EBITDA.

The value of assets in your opening balances

According to accounting standards, the value of an asset is always expressed in terms of its original actual cost and the amount of depreciation which has been applied to it. The net sum of these things is known as the 'net book value'. It is very rare in small business accounting to bother considering whether this net book value is equal to what is known as the 'net realis-able value', that is, what it could actually be sold for at this point.

More importantly, it is not acceptable to apply a *subjective* assessment to the value of an asset. I see this most often where an entrepreneur has been labouring personally for years on some plan or scheme, which they believe to have some intan-gible commercial value and they often wish to have this value expressed on their opening balance sheet. In the context of the average small business at an early stage, this isn't usually ap-propriate since such work has no actual financial cost to the business.

In addition, to be strictly correct, you should be sure that what-ever level of depreciation you are carrying forward within your opening balances is an up-to-date provision for the asset(s). Depreciation journals are rarely kept up to date in small business bookkeeping, but that said, the handling of depreciation is probably the least important aspect of your whole forecast. As long as it's broadly reasonable you'll be fine.

Capital expenditure – key points

- Make sure you understand what expenses to include as capital expenditure and what to exclude and put in your P&L. In particular, learn to recognise expenditure on intangibles such as software development which constitutes creating an asset in the business, but avoid capitalising leased or rented equipment costs. If you're in any doubt, seek professional guidance

- Understand the projected 'useful life' of your assets and establish an appropriate rate and basis on which to depreciate them. Make sure this is consistent with the way you have treated depreciation for any assets in your opening balances. Include the provision as an item in your P&L

- Do not attempt to value intangible assets (such as intellectual property) at anything other than their original financial cost without seeking professional advice

Step 5: P&L – sales revenue

For obvious reasons, projecting revenue is one of the most significant aspects of your forecast and there are a number of issues you should be aware of in addressing it.

Your revenue streams

If you had followed the advice of earlier chapters you would already have established a list of revenue streams by the time you come to think about projecting these numbers. Your chart of accounts will set out the various things for which you receive money, in a structure and level of detail which is consistent with the way you think of and discuss your business, and would present the reader with the most accessible summary of this activity.

Modelling revenue

Once you've established *what* you need to model and project, exactly *how* you go about it depends on your circumstances and objectives, your own financial and spreadsheet abilities, and/or what your chosen forecast software package will allow you to do.

The most obvious and direct way of projecting revenue is to enter a financial value or 'budget' for it – in other words, a value in pounds.

This may be adequate in some circumstances. For a very small business or a very small finance application, there may be no need for any greater complexity, and if this is true in your case you can proceed on that basis, but it has obvious limitations. Sales revenue doesn't appear from nowhere. It is almost always the product of some activity – 'so many people, doing so many things, at an average price of...' or some variation on that theme – and it is usually seen as desirable to model and show these assumptions (and calculate the revenue that results) so that both you and your audience can understand the basis of your projections and be able to assess them.

So for each of your revenue streams think about what drives it. The most common considerations are such things as:

- 'Number of units sold' x 'average price per unit'
- 'Number of active customers' x 'average spend per month'
- 'Number of active subscribers' x 'average monthly subscription fee'
- Number of new customers added in the period
- Monthly percentage growth in sales
- Level of customer 'attrition' or 'churn' in month (customers lost)
- Per cent conversion of website visitors to sale or paying subscription
- Revenue as an assumed percentage of some other revenue stream
- Sales by geographical sector or marketing 'channel'
- And so on

In particular be aware that some software can be quite restrictive about the logic it applies to what drives revenue. Forecast packages will commonly offer simple 'number of units sold' x 'average price per unit' modelling, but in practice this meets far fewer needs than might be assumed. If you are evaluating a software solution, make sure it has the flexibility to allow you to model what actually goes on in your business, rather than forcing you to bend your view of the world to meet its sometimes limited capabilities.

If you are building your own spreadsheet you are limited only by your own financial, mathematical and spreadsheet skills, but my top tips are:

- Keep it simple. It isn't the job of a forecast like this to micromanage your business. Its purpose is to tell your financial story in terms of broad financial themes and allow you to flex them. Only add detail to a financial model if it genuinely adds to either your or your reader's understanding. Don't model in fine detail things you can't really predict

- Give some thought to how you ultimately present the various drivers and assumptions you create. Make sure your reader can see what your assumptions are and how you arrived at your numbers

How optimistic or pessimistic to be?

The issue of what you should show in terms of projected revenue (and indeed in respect of everything else in your forecast) is tied up with recognising what the strategic aim of the process is. It's a very fine art and at the risk of sounding unhelpful you simply need to ask: what is more likely to persuade your reader to respond the way you want them to? Crazy optimism? Timid pessimism? In general, unless you are specifically producing a worst or best case scenario, I'd steer roughly down the middle and remember that the true purpose of your forecast is to provide a map of your financial terrain. In fact, any competent lender or investor will use your numbers as the basis of their own consideration of what may happen if things turn out better or worse.

It may also be worth reflecting that, in general, a lender is interested in *serviceability* – in getting their loan repaid – and not much in whether or not you may be a millionaire in three years' time, while an investor may be much more interested in the potential best case scenario.

Sales revenue – key points

· Make sure you present your various revenue streams in a logical way that is complete and easy to understand. Do so at an appropriate level of detail and in a way that is consistent with the way you think about and discuss your business in written plans and conversations

· Sales revenue is almost always the product of activity ('so many people, doing so many things, at an average price of…'), so make sure you model your revenue on the basis of this activity. Lenders and investors want to know how you arrive at your revenue projections

· Keep it simple. Don't overcomplicate the detail of this modelling or the variables and assumptions on which it depends, especially when these are highly speculative (as they usually are in an early stage business looking for finance)

· How optimistic or cautious your sales projections are is a matter for your own judgement, depending on your audience and your objectives

Step 6: P&L – direct costs

When we covered setting up the 'chart of accounts' we discussed how important it is to have a clear idea of your direct costs.

Direct costs will tend to fall into one of four categories (and you may not have all of them):

- Stock items or cost of goods sold – things you resell in some way, and of which you are likely to hold stock

- Obviously direct costs – like packaging, credit card costs and sales commission, which are a part of every sale and follow our rule: 'no sale, no cost'

- Direct wages and salaries – which tend to relate to staff involved in the manufacture, selling or support of your product or service

- Less justifiable direct costs – things which for some reason you wish to include as a direct cost but which don't meet our usual definition

Stock items or cost of goods sold

The general principles of modelling for stock were covered in the chapter on global considerations and we will assume that your chosen solution has an adequate provision. What is key to the issue of stock in the context of your direct costs is to ensure that you recognise the important distinction between cost of goods sold in any period, which is the figure relevant to the P&L, and the timing and cost of your purchases, which drive your cash flow. In any model which needs to address this type of cost, you need to be able to control and edit these two inputs independently.

In addition you will need to ensure that your 'closing stock' is calculated as a current asset in your balance sheet. (Opening stock, plus purchases, less costs of goods sold equals closing stock.) In practice stock models will be one of two types. Either you input the amounts you expect to purchase in any month and the model calculates the closing stock figure, or you tell the model what you expect your closing stock to be (usually as a multiple of projected revenue or how many days' stock you expect to hold) and the model automatically calculates your pattern of purchasing.

The first tends to be used where purchasing is less frequent, with greater peaks and troughs of stock levels, while the second approach is more useful when purchases are fairly continuous and likely to respond to changes in revenue patterns.

If your business involves manufacturing or assembling a large number of components to sell finished items I would advise against attempting to model exhaustive lists of such things. The result is too much data to manage, and far more than most readers are interested in or capable of appraising. Instead create sub-groups of the main types of things you deal with.

Obviously direct costs

By 'obviously' direct costs I mean those which are *clearly* true direct costs – related to sales via a clear assumption of (usually) a certain percentage of revenue. A classic example is credit card commission charges where you would assume a certain percentage as the average amount you will pay on every pound sold (which is paid for by card). It is usually straightforward to identify these costs and estimate an assumption to calculate them.

Direct wages and salaries

Even though it doesn't strictly obey the rule of being directly incurred by making a sale, direct wages are often considered to be a cost of sale and therefore included in direct costs. This happens particularly in the case of manufacturing where the labour input is clearly a direct cost of what is made and sold. Customer support staff and shop-floor staff are also often included here.

Of course by its nature this cost tends to be much more fixed, particularly in the short term and the smaller the business the less likely the cost of this input is to respond to changes in revenue on the basis of a particular cost assumption and/or levels of production and so there is an argument that this is more of an overhead. This can make achieving a consistent view of gross profitability more difficult and only you can say what is most appropriate in your circumstances.

Less justifiable direct costs

I've seen all sorts of things included in direct costs which I don't think are appropriate. This is usually because a client or their advisor comes with a preformed view of what direct costs are and they won't be budged. Sometimes it is simply because they are heavily invested in a chart of accounts in their bookkeeping which they wish to maintain and mirror (which is fair enough).

It is a matter of opinion whether this is important and the worse that results is a redefinition of what gross profit is for their particular company. In the end it is for you to decide what constitutes a logical and informative set of direct costs and therefore to communicate a clear idea of the gross profitability of what you do.

Direct costs – key points

- A well-thought-out set of direct costs creates a clear understanding of your gross profit – the inherent profitability of what you do or sell. What to include is a matter of combining common sense, convention and subjective opinion

- Direct costs tend to have a clear relationship to revenue streams according to assumptions on a percentage or per unit basis

- Direct wages are often included within direct costs but they can distort analysis of the gross profit margin because they are more fixed in their nature

Step 7: P&L – overheads

At the level of forecasting for small and medium enterprises (SMEs), projecting overheads differs from projecting revenue and direct costs because it is unlikely to be modelled on the basis of editable assumptions. Instead you will probably be entering straightforward budgets, across the months, for each line of expense.

Provided you have followed my advice and constructed a chart of accounts which sets out your overheads in a clear set of categories and at a level of detail which is appropriate for your business circumstances and your audience, you simply need to establish a realistic set of overhead budgets for what you project to achieve in operational terms.

The following are some of the common, practical issues you may encounter when dealing with projecting your overheads.

Scaling overheads

Overheads are often described as fixed costs, but in fact they differ quite a lot in the extent to which they are genuinely fixed. You may for example envisage staying in your current premises for some time to come, and be confident that your rent is contracted to remain the same over time. Your rent is indeed a fixed cost. But let's say you are also projecting to significantly increase your workforce over the same period. Is your telephone or stationery bill likely to stay the same? And your employer's liability insurance?

Be realistic about the need to scale your overhead budgets over time. Equally, be aware of how you are projecting the scale of your operation and try to avoid simply 'stepping' your overheads by a fixed percentage increase at the beginning of years two and three. Nothing works like that in the real world.

Inflation

Remember that it is the convention in small business forecasts to project on the basis of current values, that is, not to account for inflation at all. Life is much simpler this way!

Marketing budgets

The plausibility of your marketing budget in terms of the level of sales you are projecting to achieve is one of the most important elements of a forecast. Demonstrating that you understand *how* you are going to achieve your projected sales is crucial to winning the support of a lender or investor, and a clear and realistic understanding of what it will cost is a vital part of this.

Of course in some circumstances the marketing budget may not be such an important aspect, but make sure yours is clear and realistic enough to be convincing.

Payroll expenses

Most people forecast personnel costs on the basis of a figure for gross wages or salaries. Remember that you will suffer an additional cost in the form of employer's National Insurance which can add as much as 12 per cent to a salary (in practice usually a little less). Be sure to allow for this.

Remember also that every member of staff will almost certainly take around five weeks holiday a year (around 11 per cent of the total time you're paying them for), and you may incur a cost for some form of holiday cover and maybe also sickness and other absences.

In keeping with forecasting at current values, don't project annual cost of living increases, but do reflect situations where someone is paid at a deliberately suppressed rate for some period and then receives an increase.

Prepayments and accruals

There is an accounting concept known as 'prepayments' which addresses situations where an expense is paid in advance of the period to which it relates. The most common example in small businesses is the payment of rent which is often paid quarterly in advance. If you have a monthly rent cost of £1,000 but have to pay quarterly in advance, your P&L will need to reflect the monthly figure while your cash flow will need to reflect quarterly payments of £3,000.

In addition your balance sheet will need to reflect the fact that the amount by which you have paid in advance at any point is considered to be a current asset (called a prepayment). If the amounts of money are not material you may be able to ignore this subtlety of accounting but otherwise you need to be sure your software or the model you build can deal with it.

Accruals represent expenses which are incurred but not invoiced. In practice no one *projects* for accruals: you will always assume that an expense will be invoiced for. (If they occur as liabilities in your opening balances they should just be treated as trade creditors (payables).)

Depreciation

Depreciation, as an expense within your P&L, is a provision made to reflect the cost of the gradual reduction in the value of most assets. It will always be a calculation based around an assumption for the rate at which a class of asset depreciates. In almost any forecast it will be automatically calculated via a formula.

If you have assets on your books you should make sure that you are providing for depreciation. If you have previously depreciated assets in your opening balances you should forecast future depreciation on a consistent basis.

Because it is a provision, depreciation is rarely considered to be a materially important figure in small business accounting, and as long as you make a reasonable provision it will be adequate for your purposes.

Interest costs

Your business may incur interest costs if you borrow money in any form. This would include an overdraft, formal bank loans, hire purchase agreements and mortgages. You will need to ensure your software or the model you build can calculate a reasonably accurate figure for interest in any instance.

In keeping with the accounting standards which apply to interest in formal, statutory accounting, interest should be expressed as a separate line item below your operating profit or EBITDA.

Overheads – key points

- When projecting overheads you will usually be setting straightforward monetary budgets, rather than modelling them on the basis of assumptions

- Make sure that you scale your overheads realistically to reflect changing levels of commercial activity

- Be aware that overheads such as rent which may be paid for in advance will give rise to a more complex cash flow calculation, and a prepayment balance on your balance sheet

- Assuming you have at least some assets (capital expenditure) in your business make sure that an appropriate provision for depreciation is included in your overheads

- Make sure that you also include separate line items for the various sources of interest you incur when borrowing money in any form

We've all seen *Dragons' Den*. We know what happens when people don't understand their own numbers and it's never nice to watch! Know your numbers and don't hand it over to someone else.

Step 8: Debt funding – bank and other loans

If you had built a forecast that simply included the first seven steps in our ten-step process you would have created projections for a business without any funding. This is perfectly plausible in many circumstances: many businesses project to continue trading without needing any input of additional cash, from either investment or borrowing.

However, since we recognise that the most common reason for creating a forecast is to raise finance, we can assume that your numbers would probably show a shortage of cash at various points. This shortage needs to be funded and it can be done in only two ways. You either borrow it, (in some way, shape or form) or you get someone to invest it, in return for a share of the business.

For the purposes of most SME forecasts debt funding can be divided into two classes. The first is traditional bank or institutional finance, usually on a clearly structured basis. We will refer to these simply as 'bank loans'. The second is 'ad hoc' borrowing, where both the receipt and repayment of funds are likely to be subject to more variable circumstances, and may or may not be subject to interest. This would include loans from (and sometimes to) directors and associated companies ('inter-company loans') and shareholders. We will refer to these as 'directors' loans' as this is the most common source of ad hoc borrowing for a small business.

Borrowing has implications for all three parts of your forecast (the P&L, cash flow and balance sheet), and you need to make sure that your forecast handles them correctly. Note especially that the interest incurred on a loan is the only aspect which impacts your P&L. This is the expense to your business of borrowing money. Crucially, the receipt of loan funds is *not* revenue to the business and repayments are *not* a cost to your business *within your P&L*. Instead, the receipt of loan funds and the repayments you make are part of your cash flow. Last, your balance sheet will need to reflect the liability you have for any loan at any point, which is the sum of what you originally borrowed, plus any interest expense which has accrued, less any payment you have made in total.

In the event that you are projecting to lend money to anyone, these rules simply work in reverse.

Bank loans

The most common form of bank borrowing is a standard capital and interest repayment loan which is characterised by having a fixed term for the repayment (usually expressed as a number of months) and an agreed interest rate (which may or may not be fixed over the agreed term). This structure would include most standard bank loans, hire purchase agreements and mortgages.

Occasionally loans may be taken which are subject to less standard terms, for example 'interest-only repayments' (with a later single repayment of the capital sum) or 'repayment holidays'. Most forecast software will deal with the most common types; non-standard loans almost always need to be modelled individually.

One of the most common stress tests that a bank will perform on projections when considering making a loan is to flex the numbers for increased interest rates to see if the business would still be able to afford the repayments. If you are seeking variable rate borrowing from a bank, you need to consider whether your model needs to allow you to do this yourself.

If you are building your own model for bank loans, it is important to understand how interest is calculated and accrued on such a loan. You will need to research a concept, known as 'rule of 78' or 'sum of digits', which dictates that the total interest you pay for a loan is not evenly distributed over the term. (The interest cost of a fixed repayment loan is larger in the short term and reduces over time.) You can see the effect of this in the bank loan interest shown in the P&L on our demonstration forecast report (www.edgeforecast.co.uk/demo).

Sales invoice financing (invoice factoring or discounting)

Sales invoice financing, often referred to as either 'invoice factoring' or 'invoice discounting', is a form of funding which advances cash against the issue of sales invoices, making funds available that would otherwise be subject to the delay of normal customer credit terms. The specifics of the terms and conditions differ from scheme to scheme, but in forecasting terms they are quite similar. To all intents and purposes, an invoice finance facility is an account with an overdraft facility, the limit on which is set as a percentage of the total you are owed by customers at any point.

I have never yet seen forecast software (apart from mine) which deals automatically with this issue, so if you need to forecast an invoice finance arrangement you will inevitably need to create your own model to deal with it. Unfortunately, it is beyond our scope to discuss the details of it here.

'Trade finance' or 'purchase line'

These forms of funding relate to bank facilities which fund the purchase of stock and they are often also associated with sales invoice arrangements. They are invariably complex to model and you will be highly unlikely to find such functionality in forecast software. Again, if you need to model this kind of funding you will need to create your own.

Directors' (and other) ad hoc loans

Sometimes you (or, more specifically, your business) may borrow money from sources other than banks and institutions and these loans are likely to be taken and repaid on a more flexible and individual basis.

The most common source of this type of loan is the company's directors, but it would also include loans to or from shareholders, associated companies or any other person or entity with whom you might come to such an arrangement.

What is different about modelling this type of loan is that both the receipt of funds and the repayments are likely to be subject to an ad hoc schedule, and therefore less likely to be governed by a formulaic approach. Instead you will probably enter these transactions directly and you may or may not need to model interest.

Such loans may also involve lending, as opposed to borrowing funds (as in the classic overdrawn directors' loan account), in which case the general rules are reversed. Interest you earn will be part of your revenue for P&L purposes and the loan balance will be an asset rather than a lability.

You should be particularly careful to make directors' loans highly transparent in your forecast, since this is an area which is of keen interest to lenders and investors – relating as it does to the financial relationship between the business and its principals.

Loan accounts in your opening balances

If you have pre-existing loan liabilities in your opening balances, you will need to project the future movements (usually repayments) on the loan. Particularly in the case of bank loans you need to ensure that your bookkeeping is up to date with the bank's statement balance and that you have posted the correct amount of interest to date in your historic P&L. If not, you'll find it difficult to reconcile your loan model to the likely reality.

Debt funding – key points

- Debt funding (borrowing money) is one of two ways to fund your business
- You need to be able to model both formal structured bank loans, and ad hoc directors' and other loans
- It's important to understand how various aspects of a loan relate to P&L, cash flow and balance sheet
- Forecasting the future behaviour of existing loans depends on a correct accounting position within your opening balances

"

Too much and too little information are the twin enemies of understanding and communication. If a detail helps, put it in. But if it doesn't contribute to either, leave it out.

"

Step 9: Investment and dividends

Investment

If you need funding but you don't want to *borrow* money your only solution is to attract investment.

For our purposes we will consider the straightforward issue of ordinary shares in a business – selling a simple percentage of the ownership of your business, and ultimately sharing any future profit with those shareholders. Many complexities arise in this aspect of corporate finance but they are not common in SME businesses and do not concern us here.

In handling investment in your forecast you should be aware that:

- Investment funds have no bearing on P&L. Investment income should never appear in your P&L

- Investment funds are clearly a significant aspect of your cash flow and they will always be matched by an equivalent entry on your balance sheet (usually referred to as 'equity' or 'share capital' which shows the total amount that has been invested in your business). If all you have in terms of investment in your business to date is your original subscriber shares, which might be as little as £1, this is no less subject to this rule. You will have £1 of share capital on your balance sheet

- It is probably more common when seeking investment to create projections which assume this money will be raised and therefore show a funded position. On the other hand, some people prefer to show the overdrawn cash balance, without the funding, to identify the extent of the funding gap. There are no clear rules on this

- In general the kind of forecast we are discussing has no need to manage the issue of individual percentage owner-ships in the business. It is only concerned with the amount of money that has been invested in total. Nor does any no-tion of 'share premium' (the value paid for a share above its nominal value), have any bearing. This is an outmoded concept in any case

Dividends

When someone invests in a business they usually hope it will go on to make a profit! If so, those profits may be distributed to the shareholders, in cash, through what is known as 'dividends', and if you are forecasting profits you may wish to project these payments.

Just as with investment, dividends have no bearing on your P&L. They are merely projected entries in your cash flow and the equivalent entry will be to reduce the value of the retained profits you have on your balance sheet.

A forecast will not generally concern itself with any ultimate 'exit' or sale of the business. The end point of a forecast is merely a projected accounting position at the end of a period of trading.

Nor does it in general attempt to establish a return on investment or a valuation for the business, which is a process subject to a wide range of methods and approaches.

Investment and dividends – key points

- If you are forecasting for the purpose of attracting investment funds it is usual to include these funds in your cash flow forecast and show the funded position
- Investment and dividends relate only to cash flow and balance sheet. They have no bearing on P&L
- Your core forecast will not generally be expected to deal with return on investment, a potential exit or future valuation

Step 10: Publishing reports

At some point after having cycled through the previous nine steps, probably many times, you will end up with a final set of numbers that you wish to share with the world. Well done!

But sadly you haven't quite finished. You have yet to publish and distribute this information to those who want to read it. This after all is substantially why you did it in the first place: to give people the information they have demanded.

It never ceases to amaze me how much effort people can put into producing forecasts while so completely neglecting this last, vital stage of the process. When I was responsible for reviewing all the financial information that was submitted to Crowdcube for their crowdfunding pitches, it was not uncommon for people to have saved their spreadsheets as PDF files which were actually completely illegible, either on screen or when printed. The idea that anyone might actually want to read this information seemed to have escaped them!

What you need to achieve in respect of the reports you publish from your forecast is largely a matter of common sense. You may be constrained by what your chosen software will allow you to do or by your own practical skills and knowledge in the matter, but here are a set of simple guidelines to aim at.

Create a financial executive summary

Just like a written plan, a set of financials needs an executive financial summary with all the essential information on a single page. Be aware, however, that forecasting software is often not great at this. For example, the software most commonly used by professional accountants produces reports which have no such summary and requires the reader to wade through every single page to extract the high-level information they need.

If you're using proprietary software you'll have to live with what they give you, but if you're building your own make sure you create an executive summary report which brings all the information together in a digestible format.

The right amount of information

Ask your lender or investor specifically what they want. Ask them whether they want the background detail behind whichever parts of the core P&L, cash flow and balance sheet numbers they have asked you for and don't give it to them if they don't want it. You may have slaved over the fine print of what you've done, and that may have been important, but your reader may only want the essentials. Especially if they need to produce a printed copy!

Good structure, layout and labelling

Remember, even if it's likely to be read on screen, you are essentially publishing a document. To be useful – and to get your reader on your side! – you need to make life easy for them. So make sure that you:

- observe the conventional accounting format of P&L, cash flow and balance sheet, *in that order*

- try to keep individual pages of the report to a single page where possible

- label your pages clearly so they know which bit of your forecast they're looking at (a P&L report can appear much like a cash flow report until you look closely at it…)

- make your date ranges clear and very obvious

- provide a contents page so they know what's in the report.

While you're at it maybe add your logo to the document if you can and generally take the trouble to make a good impression. Lenders and investors are only human (usually!) and are as susceptible as anyone else to good impressions!

Legibility

It may sound obvious but make sure your document is actually legible. Do not put too much information on one page in a very small font size. In general, if something is not easy to read when printed it is not easy to read on screen either, even if you do use some kind of 'zoom' function, because you tend to lose sight of row and column headings on which a lot of financial reports depend.

Always look at it both on screen and when printed and make an objective judgement about how it looks. There's nothing more annoying, especially for us oldies, than having to squint at numbers to read them!

File format

Unless you are specifically asked for an editable copy of your source spreadsheet, always produce your reports as a properly paginated PDF file. Most people do not find it easy to trawl through spreadsheets to garner information. However familiar you are with the layout of your model having worked on it for ages, a spreadsheet will be less transparent and user-friendly to your reader than you think.

Publishing reports – key points

· What your information looks like *matters*. Remember you're producing these numbers for someone to look at and appraise, so make their life easy, not hard, and make a good impression on them

· Use your common sense and adopt good practices around producing your reports

· Find out specifically what information your lender or investor wants and give them only this; not more because you think it looks clever!

· Reports should be easily legible both on screen and when printed, and sensibly structured and easy to follow

· Produce your reports as PDF files and only give people your source spreadsheet if they specifically ask for it

About Edge Forecast

Numbers really not your thing? There's a faster, smarter way to create your forecast!

There are many ways to achieve the high standards of robust, professional, financial forecasts discussed in this book, but few of them avoid a good deal of financial understanding, effort and general head-scratching on your part.

There is, however, one solution which can save you a huge amount of time and pain, and will guarantee the outcome.

The author's business, Edge Forecast, provides a unique service via telephone and screen share to create tailored, editable forecasts for clients all over the UK (and indeed the world).

This service has a proven track record since 2011 and has helped businesses like yours successfully raise many millions of pounds of finance. Edge Forecast offers a highly flexible range of packages, suitable for businesses of all sizes and for all types of fundraising and general business planning. Most forecasts are delivered same day.

If you'd like to know more about this fast and affordable way to meet all of the standards and benchmarks promoted in this book *automatically*, without having to address each and every one individually, you can learn more about it at www.edgeforecast.co.uk or call Edge Forecast on 01225 438438.

About the author

Simon Thompson came to financial forecasting as a speciality after a long and varied career that encompassed alternating bouts of entrepreneurship and accountancy. As a result he has an unusual breadth of commercial experience encompassing businesses of all sizes in many sectors.

His current business, Edge Forecast, provides a unique mix of expertise and specialist software to create tailored, editable forecast models for small and medium businesses and he works with many organisations and platforms who provide or advise on finance and growth for SMEs.

He lives with his wife Clare in Bath, supports whoever is currently leading the premiership from the comfort of his sofa and litter makes him furious.

Also by Authority Guides

The Authority Guide to Marketing Your Business Book: 52 easy-to-follow tips from a book PR expert

Chantal Cooke

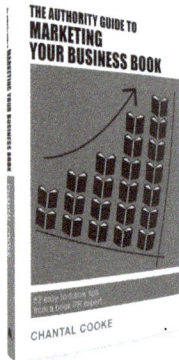

Want to get your business book flying off the shelves?

It's never too soon to start thinking about how to market and promote your book. In this Authority Guide, leading book PR and marketing expert Chantal Cooke, presents 52 tips that will make your book stand out from the crowd, build your credibility as an author, and ensure you achieve those all-important sales.

EU Safety Representative: euComply OÜ Pärnu mnt 139b-14 11317 Tallinn
Estonia hello@eucompliancepartner.com +33 756 90241

www.ingramcontent.com/pod-product-compliance
Lightning Source LLC
Chambersburg PA
CBHW061052200326
41520CB00027BA/7521